POETIC THOUGHTS

Fresh POETIC THOUGHTS

FELIX CRUZ

To order additional copies of this book, contact:
Xlibris Corporation
1-888-795-4274
www.Xlibris.com
Orders@Xlibris.com
130349

Contents

Dedication

This book is dedicated to special people like Sylvia, Felix (the 3rd), Anthony, Christopher, and Andrew. These individuals are the ones that inspire me to write and to be successful in everything I do.

May God bless them and protect them always.

Sincerely
Felix

3 Yet One

Water, Ice, Water Vapor,
Three sides of a triangle,
Life, liberty, pursuit of happiness,
World of God, the world of the Kingdom, and the world of Creation,
Impermanence, suffering, and no-self,
Body, Soul, and Spirit,
Father, Son, and Holy Ghost,
Protons, neutrons, electrons,
Me, myself, and I,
Elohim, though 3 yet One,
So as we reflect on these,
It is plain to see that,
3 is yet One.

A Friend is

Worth more than rubies untold,
Always there for you in time of need,
One who looks beyond your faults and
Sees your pain without looking for gain,
The one you look for in times of trouble,
A Comforting presence, word of assurance,
An encouraging word, a helping hand,
The one who stands by you no matter what,
The one who will give you their last dollar,
The one without hypocritical thoughts or acts,
One who will never lie to you even if it hurts,
That person who will give up their life for you
Without thinking about it twice,
How nice it is to have a friend!
Acquaintances are easy to find, Oh! But true
Friends are sometimes hard to find—
Oh! What a friend I have in Jesus!!
He can be your friend too—He's nearby.

A Mother's Love

Before the beginning of the world I was conceived and forged by the miracle of God; The reality of my life was made visible in my mother's womb. For nine months I lived within the warmth of her body, waiting for that day when the light from the world would shine on me.

Oh! How happy and full of love a mother is at this time; when she first sees and touches the fruit of her labor. All the pain and discomfort she felt seems like it was all a dream, a dream which now has come true.

A mother's love will nurse and establish the newborn, angelic like baby, so that it can cope in this unpredictable world.

A mother's love is the life blood that motivates us to be the person which we ought to be.

So now we've grown up and throughout all this time, mother has always been there to lend a helping hand, reaching out with all the love that we all need so much.

A mother's love is like a treasure which is given to us from the first day we're born. This treasure was fully given to us to care for and to always possess.

Oh! All the money in the world cannot compare to a mother's love, so pure and limitless. It has no boundaries for it was put there by God in his image.

To every mother in the world, I salute you.

To my mother, I love you now and forever.

A Seed

Unless a seed dies it
Cannot bring forth many
More seeds like itself—
The love of this cosmos
Will only lead to the loss
Of eternal life.
Love not the world neither
The things that are in the world.
Die to selfishness and to the
The pride of life,
Humble yourself, crucify the flesh
And God will lift you up.
Be a good steward and plant
The seed of faith without doubt,
God will nurture that seed until
The time of reaping and harvesting.
The fields are ripe, it's time to reap.

A *Song of* Love

The *birds* awakened me with their beautiful morning song,
As I lay *nest* to you my heart feels glad within me,
So full of love for you, my love

That my words cannot define the divines of your tenderness,
So soft, so warm, so exciting! My heart is in ecstasy,
Ecstasy, Oh! Yes, to be in your arms, caressing, touching, and
exploding,

Oh! What a sensation. It's always good, even better than the best,
I'm in love like I've never been before
You are the ultimate of women,

A song of love for you, my darling, I have tried to write for you,
But, you see—there are no words to define what's in
my heart for you.

A Song of Praise

A song of praise I sing to you Oh, Lord,
My heart rejoices in your presence and
Your praise is forever in my heart,

Jesus, the very mention of your name,
Brings gladness to my soul,
Oh, such fullness of joy, like rivers of
Living water flowing in me and through me,

A new song have you put in my mouth,
A song of praise and worship that only
Jesus deserves; for there is no other like you,
My Jesus.

My spirit will praise you from this day,
From this day forth and forevermore.

All In a Day's Time

Woke up this morning trying to rush to make it to work on time,
It's all in a day's time!!
Didn't feel all that good but what could I do,
It's all in a day's time!!
I psyched myself up to cope with the world,
And with all the things I would face today,
It's all in a day's time!!
I finally got dressed and all pressed,
And said so long to my wife,
It's all in a day's time!!
Rushed to the bus, relaxed a bit
It's all in day's time!!
Got to the train it all seemed so vain,
But all the time I knew,
It's all in day's time!!
Made it to work, worked really hard,
Had fun doing it,
It's all in day's time!!
Worked overtime to make a little extra cash,
It's all in a day's time!!
I relaxed again coming home on the train,
Nodded for a while and before I knew it,
Reached Fordham Road,
It's all in a day's time!!
Finally was home, Home Sweet Home,
Oh! How good it feels to be home,
It's all in a day's time

All is Vanity

If I gain all the riches in the world,
What does it profit me?
If I have all wisdom and knowledge,
Can I turn back the hands of time?
When I look in the mirror,
Can I recall what I really look like?
It all seems so vain—
Can it take away the pain and suffering?
Nevertheless, we must persevere
And look to the heavens
Without disdain but with hope.
In the end, we will prevail.

All Is Well in a Dry Place

There can be no life without water,
Even in the desert there is water,
An oasis where your thirst can be quenched
Can be found in a dry and weary land.
An ever-flowing well springing up into
Everlasting life is there to be found—
We should try to dig our own wells,
Or unclog the wells of our forefathers,
Once we have our well, we must draw out
All the blessings of life that is deep within.
Continuous drawing and flowing of the water,
Must be our mission while in submission
To the purposes and leading of the one from
Whom the water flows—this well will never,
Run dry—find or dig your well, then you,
Can say all is well with me.

Am I My Brother's Keeper?

What is the highest love?
But to give your life for a friend,
Who is a friend you may ask?
Is it the homeless we pass by?
Is it the sick and the helpless?
Is it the orphans and widows?
Is it those behind prison walls?
There is so much need, yet so,
Much greed,
Who shall I send to the nations?
We are all brothers from the start,
To keep each other from all harm,
Am I my brother's keeper?
You may ask,
Yes you are, Yes you are,
Dare to try?

An Heir Looms

Inside the womb an heir looms,
Being weaved by our Maker,
From eternal members that were
Created before time existed.
The first born destined to inherit
All that the king has consisted,
Heirlooms, the dynasty will be his,
The right of birth has come,
The passage from eternity to time,
The heir still looms in our presence,
Bearing the essence and smell of incense,
That signals royalty which demands loyalty.

As a Man Thinks

As a man thinks in his heart so is he,
Does a grasshopper know it's a grasshopper?
Does a lion know he's a lion?
Does a man or woman know their potential?

The kingdom of God is in you,
If you are one of His,
Imagine how much potential there is,
When all power is given unto you,

Visions of greatness are possible,
Think big with positive thoughts,
Verbalize your dreams,
Be proactive and redeem the time,

God gave us dominion to rule on earth,
To declare His wisdom and power,
To do great exploits for the kingdom,
We are complete and perfect in Him,

Don't think you're a grasshopper,
Be a lion, you can do it,
I'm not lying.

Be Still and Know that I Am God

Why are you cast down, Oh my soul?
"Trust in me", saith your God.
Don't worry about tomorrow,
For the things of tomorrow will take
Care of themselves,
We rush here
We rush there
Sometimes it seems like you're not there,
But you always let me know you care,
Great is thy faithfulness, Oh, Lord,
Teach me not to fret
But in everything, looking
Unto the hills from whence
Cometh my help
My help cometh from the Lord,
Your thoughts are forever upon me,
You created me, you redeemed me,
Therefore, you will sustain me,
Thank you Lord, for your
Tender and everlasting mercies,
Teach me to wait upon you Lord,
Search my heart and purify it,
Try my thoughts and cleanse them.
Teach me to be still and to
Know that you are God
Forever and ever with me.

Because I Love You

Someone special, that's what you are to me,
Together, we are one,
That's how it should be
My love for you is so deep,
I have visions of you while I sleep,
If we should part, I'll remember us,
But these memories would blow away like dust,
People would be surprised to see us part,
If you ever leave me, it will break my heart,
I really need you in my life,
As you read what I've written,
Believe it is true,
All that I feel is just LOVE FOR YOU

Bitter Sweet

I met a man named Bitter Sweet,
Who went through life on two limp feet,
Each waking day that passed him by,
Could not restore his faith in I,
What a bitter thing it is to taste,
The Sweetness of love made in haste,
There is no time to waste,
No time to hesitate,
Cold becomes hot,
First we go down,
Then we come up,
New becomes old,
Old is renewed,
Left becomes right,
As right as can be,
Now is now later,
This moment in time,
Presently headed forward,
While still living then,
Bitter is now Sweet,
A man must confess.

Conscience

Revelations of the inner self,
Indentations in our mind,
Of all the experiences and thoughts,
As we travel through time and space,
What's right and what's wrong,
Our conscience knows,
Before the foundations of the world,
Our conscience was formed,
A choice we were given,
To choose the way we should walk,
One road leads to life,
Another leads to strife,
Choose life and not death,
Live life with a clean conscience,
To reach the pinnacle of your destiny

Consumed

Organic tissue so beautifully,
Composed—Compressed—and Forged,
Heat-treated Pressed Down,
Annealed Revealed,
Back in the Heart-h,
Where Impurities are cleansed,
By the overwhelming Fire,
Refined—Defined,
Fuel for the Fire,
Life endures—Conjures,
Devouring Energies,
Conserved—Converted,
TRANSFORMATION,
Different strata and Dimensions,
Consumed, Elevated,
To Higher Energy Levels

LIFE LIVES ON...

Declarations

Write down your vision
And declare it,
Declaration—
If you write it down it will
Surely come to pass.
God spoke the Word and
Wrote it and declared it,
It will surely come to pass—
Write down your dreams and
Visions and run with them.
God will do the rest.
He will bring them to pass.

Destiny

**Destined to be,
All I can be,
Predestined? Maybe,
Choices to make,
Of what lays ahead,
Don't be afraid,
Stay on the road,
To success,
That will eventually,
Impress**

Duality

A man cannot serve
Two masters
He will either hate the one
And love the other
You are either against
Or for something
It is either hot or cold
It is either near or far
It is either low or high
Darkness or light prevails
Death or alive
Male or female
Afraid or unafraid
A leader or a follower
Particle or wave
A wise man or a fool
Duality defines the
Quality of our being
Belief or unbelief
I choose to belief

Equations

Variables are strange animals
They can evolve into many shapes and forms
In fact, they may take on any value
They are the very essence of formulas
And even of expressions
Which express themselves sometimes in small terms, defining large
ideas
The very nature of our universe can be defined with equations
Theories can be mathematically spoken in no uncertain terms
Relatively speaking, that is, infinitesimal quantities equating something
yet
Unknown or quite not understood
Predicting processes or events which cannot be seen with the naked eye
Equations are solutions to unsolvable queries
This balance must be maintained
Always reminding ourselves that something or nothing cannot be
divided by nothing
Otherwise the very thing we are trying to define becomes indefinable
and unsolvable
"String Theory" or "Theory of Everything" can be equated be defining
things
Unknown in many dimensions not easily visualized
Even travel through time warps is possible
Equations give us solutions to the real and unreal universal
transgressions.

Evolution of the Blues

Born south of the Mason-Dixon Line,
Created by itinerant black musicians,
Traveling from honky-tonks, farms,
Work-camps, and even roadhouses.
The wayfarer crying out with rhythms
That echoed the melodies and harmonies
That celebrated birth, death, and religion.
Slave songs and field hollers, chants, shouts,
And yells spread along the Mississippi.
Through roust-abouts while looking for work—
Freedmen and ex-slaves freeing their intellect
And creative essence that lead back to their roots.
Clarinets, tubas, trombones, guitars, harmonicas,
Were adopted like children who were homeless
And needed to reveal their woes and experiences.
Pentatonic scales that repeat progressions of chords
That is so simple but yet so revealing of that
Human longing for freedom and sense of belonging.
Blue is the color of the blood that lies within
And becomes red when exposed to the melodic
Sounds of a blues song sung from the heart.

Façade

Surreptitious reflections in a two-way mirror,
Bouncing back to me all to unclear,
Like looking through a glass darkly,
Melodious tunes that I'm unable to hear,

Distorted visions that seem so real,
Yet unfathomable from all dimensions,
Time warps in the spatial lattice,
Created by inner construed elusive dissensions,

A sense of self in tension,
That seemingly brings pleasure,
Façade is the face we add,
To the myriad of expressions,

That we treasure

Faith

Seeing is believing someone said,
Or if I could touch it,
Someone said instead,

The substance of things hoped for
The evidence of things not seen,
Things that are ARE made of
things
Not seen;

Contradiction or premonition,
Neither one someone said,
Is the air seen or heard,

Can the naked eye see the
Inner mysteries of an atom
Or follow the path of an electron;

Are quarks a quirk?

When a tree falls in the forest
Do you hear the sound?
What is a vacuum? Is it
Made up of empty space?

Is the number zero? Nothing
At all—Or does it represent
A quantity not yet understood;

Is it possible to make something
Out of nothing?
Does a thought become real or
Does reality generate thought?
Can we get our hands on wisdom,
on

Honesty, on integrity, on Love, on
Friendship?
Is it possible that believing on
Something can make that
something
Become real,

Can the mere utterance of words
Generate a chain-reaction which
Energizes and solidifies those
Things invisible into a substance
Made visible

Are things visible merely a
reflection
Of the invisible? Or is reality
merely
The manifestation of what always
was,

Faith can be a powerful force that
has
Creative powers,

Faith causes The Foreordained
Attributes
Inside our minds
To become the
Here and now.
If we speak it and believe it,
It will come to pass.

Fruits of the Spirit

Be fruitful and multiply,
God commanded mankind,
What is being fruitful?
Is it merely procreation?
Or is it more than that?
But the fruit of the Spirit is love,
Joy, peace, patience,
Kindness, goodness, faithfulness,
To be fruitful is to desire these fruits,
What a different world it would be,
If mankind would possess these fruits,
So that we can love our neighbor,
As we love ourselves,
So that we can do unto others,
As we want them to do unto us,
So that we can make a difference,
And bring about positive change,
Fruits are beautiful and tasty,
You can be beautiful and tasty too.

Full of Words

Be Grateful
Be Thankful
Be Joyful
Be Peaceful
Be Wonderful
Be Plentiful
Be Bountiful
Be Thoughtful
Be Helpful
Be Tactful
Be Fruitful
Be Cheerful
Be Powerful
Be Respectful
Be Merciful
Don' be Hateful
Don't be Spiteful
Be Godfull

Games People Play

The world is a stage
And we are merely actors
That play the method acting
Parts that our lives demand,
Some are horror and some
Have honor, some are tragedies
While others are romantic comedies
Full of melodrama accompanied by
Musical overtones of exaggerated
Emotional outbursts—
It's all part of the games people play
Where there are no rules or referees,
May the best man win—
It's not whether you win or lose,
But how you win.

Generations

Baby Boomer cries out
We must bring about social
Change, the status quo cannot
Remain—
Gen X replies, in a jaded, cynical
Overtone, everything is Retro-Kitsch,
Gen Y counterpunches, the world is
An ideal and honest place
Where self parody is commonplace
While listening to NSync and Timberlake
On Apple Ipod, while still being optimistic—
The stock market is up.
Gen Z is hiding behind the World Wide Web,
Afraid to be upclose and personal,
A netgeneration reaching globally
In a nanosecond of instant messaging
That forever unites us.
Digital Communities of harmony and love.

God is Light

God is Light and there is no darkness in Him—
He wears light as a garment,
His word is a lamp unto our feet,
And a light for our path.
I am translated form darkness to the Light,
When I believe in Him, I walk in His light,
So let your light shine in the midst of a
Perverse and wicked generation that is
Looking for light but are walking in darkness.
Jesus is the Light of the world,
We are in Him and He is in us,
Let your light so shine upon this world,
That the world might see your good deeds
And give glory to the Father who is in heaven.
If your eyes are good, then your whole being
Will be full of light,
No one lights a light and hides it, let your light
So shine so that darkness will dissipate all around
You.
In Him was life, and that life was the light of men.
The Light shines in darkness, but the darkness
Does not understand it.
The true Light that gives light to every man
Has come into the world,
That Light is Jesus, step into Light and receive
The Light of life.

Haiti's Quake

Why so much suffering and pain?
For those struggling, when it seems
It's all in vain—
Crushed by the weight of stubble
When all around me is trouble,
All alone in pain, no water, no sustenance.
It's dark all around me,
Where are my loved ones?
All I do is think about them
And pray to God to save them—
"Don't be afraid of death"
A survivor sings as she is pulled
From darkness to light.
"I feel good", a young boy answers
When asked, how you feel?
After six days of captivity.
What lesson can be learned?
Is it that we should not fret
About earthly things?
Is it that life is like smoke?
It's here for a little while
But then it's gone.
Is it that we should build up treasures
In heaven not on earth?
Heaven and Earth shall pass away,
But our spirit lives forever...
Look to Jesus for eternal life,
Ashes to ashes, dust to dust,
But our spirit shall be joined
With Him as we pass from
This life to eternity.
So sing in the midst of tragedy,
Our body and possessions can be
Crushed, but our spirit will always
Remain, No more pain.
Hallelujah!

He Never Sleeps

Who has been His counselor?
Does He ever hunger or thirst?
He is forever thinking about us,
His thoughts upon us are more,
Than we can number,
He never slumbers,
This knowledge is too great for me,
I cannot fathom it,
Call upon Him, Don't be afraid,
To wake Him, Cause He never sleeps,
And He never slumbers

Heart, Mind, Lips

From the abundance of the heart,
The mouth speaks,
As a man thinks so is He,
Thoughts from the mind,
Are inscribed in our hearts,
From the heart to the neurons,
Synoptic Synapses fired up,
Signal our vocal chords to react,
Lips form the words that create,
The reality within to become real,
Words that have substance,
And are forever recorded in,
Our surroundings, later to be,
Replayed for all to hear,
Vibrating strings that will sing,
Of what was in our hearts

Parallel Universes

A dual existence we live,
What I see now may not,
Be really all that there is,
If I could cross over to the,
Other side, my fears may then,
Subside, My destiny awaits me,
There, so close and yet so far,
As close as an electron is to the,
Nucleus, parallel and yet so distant,
A parallel universe, I need to traverse,
To see who I really am,
This journey someday I will take,
Yet there is no haste, no waste,
A dual existence which I can taste

Snowflakes

Like complex crystals
We are all different.
DNA lattice structures
Crystalline structures—
Coalesced together in an
Infinite number of compositions.
Each being unique and special—
Beautiful creations worthy of
Admiration, from dust to dust,
Created in the heavens,
Seen on earth forever
Creating the wonder of beauty.

Towers of Power

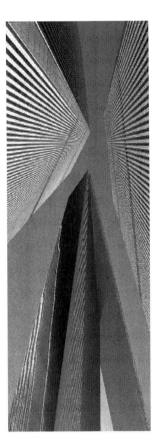

Symbols of America's
strength
Reaching out to the
heavens
Although they've
fallen down
Will always remain as
TOWERS OF POWER
So many lives have
been lost
And many hearts so
distraught
From the ruins and
rubble
Will arise hope in the
midst of struggle
The sleeping giant
has awakened

To take revenge
against the evil doers
Our stars and stripes
so majestic and
beautiful
Will serve to remind
us that united we
stand
And divided we fall
All for one and one
for all
As TOWERS OF
POWER we march to
war
And in the end the
terror is gone
God bless us all.

Wisdom

The fear of God is the beginning of wisdom,
Wisdom calls out to us from the heavens,
It is more precious than gold or silver,
It is better to have wisdom than all riches,

To gain understanding and wisdom is my desire,
To be able to know the mysteries of God,
And the riches of his mercy is my goal,
Ask and it shall be given unto you,
Believing that you will receive it,

Through wisdom God stretched out the heavens,
By wisdom He created all things,
Wisdom is the means, by which we get to know Him,
So don't be afraid and ask for it

Made in the USA
Middletown, DE
13 May 2022